Published by: **Sourcebooks, Inc.**
P.O. Box 372, Naperville, Illinois, 60566
(708) 961-3900
FAX: (708) 961-2168

Editorial: Todd Stocke
Cover Design: Wayne Johnson
Interior Design: Wayne Johnson, Sourcebooks, Inc.
Production: Corey Dean

ISBN: 1-57071-036-8

Printed and bound in the United States of America.
10 9 8 7 6 5 4 3 2 1

BREATHING
SPACE

A Journal
For Women
Who Do Too Much

From the bestselling book
Finding Time
by Paula Peisner

 Sourcebooks, Inc.
Naperville, IL

"Life is made up of desires that seem big and vital one minute, and little and absurd the next. I guess we get what's best for us in the end."

—Alice Caldwell Rice

"I must govern the clock, not be governed by it."

—Golda Meir

Develop ways for family members to contribute to household chores such as cooking, cleaning, grocery shopping, doing laundry and running errands.

"One doesn't recognize in one's life the really important moments—not until it's too late."

—Agatha Christie

_____

_____

_____

_____

_____

_____

_____

A cushion of comfort pads you in the right place.
Always extend your estimate of the time that's
required to reach your goal.

O Bird of Time
   on your fruitful bough,
What are the songs you sing?

   —Sarofini Naidu
   "The Bird of Time"

It's not enough just to fit fun in. Fun should be a priority, and it should be scheduled.

The phone does not have to be a time thief if you limit its access to you and learn to control conversations.

Do the worst first.

_____

_____

_____

_____

_____

_____

_____

Only when we accept the right to set boundaries can we live our lives on our own terms.

_____

_____

_____

_____

_____

_____

_____

Make a list of your responsibilities, activities, and commitments, and decide which ones you can eliminate, share, modify, or reduce. Think about who you need to talk to to make it happen. Then, just do it.

"Don't agonize, organize."

–Florynce R. Kennedy

Don't burden yourself with loose ends. Loose ends only steal your time.

Create mini-breaks in your routine that take your mind off the immediate priority and let you recharge your batteries.

Listen carefully. Before you respond, understand what the other person expects from you—and consider your own priorities before you commit to someone else.

Do a 'to do' list daily. Don't write a new list everyday; just update the previous one.

Recognize your limitations and your priorities.
Simplify your life. You'll enjoy it more.

Just do it—

inspiration will follow.

"Learn to get in touch with silence within yourself and know that everything in this life has a purpose. There are no mistakes, no coincidences. All events are blessings given to us to learn from."

–Elizabeth Kubler-Ross

Talk to a friend or relative who will listen, who has been there before and has similar demands and responsibilities.

Instead of focusing on an activity that doesn't really require your complete physical and mental attention, try doing two things at once.

_____

_____

_____

_____

_____

_____

_____

When someone else can do it, delegate it.

_____

_____

_____

_____

_____

_____

_____

No one can get you to better use your time on this earth. It's up to you. If you want to enjoy life more, you can.

31

"I think knowing what you
cannot do is more important
than knowing what you can do.
In fact, that's good taste."

—Lucille Ball

Allowing your family to take care of themselves gives you time to take care of yourself. Don't feel guilty about this. You deserve some nurturing. After all, if you don't take care of yourself, no one else will. You're worth it.

Try to combine activities to simultaneously get things done and save time.

Set aside time to make outgoing calls. By initiating the call, you
will be better prepared and can control its pace and content.

 Work backwards, plan ahead.

_____

_____

_____

_____

_____

_____

_____

Look out a day, a few weeks, even a month or so in advance. Create a picture of what needs to get done, how it should be done, and what you can do today. Make it a habit to repeat this mental exercise regularly.

Get accustomed to scheduling all of your time. Give your own personal enjoyment a high priority. Plan ahead and schedule it.

"... When you finish with a job it is wiser to make the break completely. Cut off the old life, clean and sharp. If your mind is tired, that is the only way. If your mind is lively, you will soon find other interests."

–Caroline Le Jeune

Pad all your time estimates and you'll avoid being late, rushing unnecessarily, and disappointing someone.

Maintain your calendar in a regularly visible place. Update it throughout the day. Inform others of changes.

Solitude and quiet offer opportunities for reflection and rejuvenation. Everybody deserves rest. Even God rested, working six days and resting one.

_____

_____

_____

_____

_____

_____

_____

_____

Make it a habit to check your messages and get back to people immediately.

Learn to manage other's
expectations and corresponding
perceptions.

"It would be good to find some quiet inlet where the waters were still enough for reflection, where one might sense the joy of the moment, rather than plan breathlessly for a dozen mingled treats in the future."

–Kathleen Norris
"Bread Into Roses"

Leave your answering machine on to screen calls, or have your secretary screen them for you.

Trust discipline and not your memory. You've got too much going on, so keep records.

_____

_____

_____

_____

_____

_____

_____

You can be all that you are capable of and still keep your sanity by setting some limits and re-adjusting your assumptions.

_____

_____

_____

_____

_____

_____

_____

We probably spend more time worrying about what
we should do than doing what we want to do.

"Then give to the world the best you have, and the best will come to you."

–Madeline Bridges
"Life's Mirror"

Tie up loose ends by telling yourself and those involved that you have completed your end. Anything else needed will have to be handled as a new project, question, or favor.

Spend some quiet time alone and let your mind wander. In a relaxed state, you will be surprised how your subconscious mind can be a positive vehicle for change.

Try to consciously train your mind to work backwards, so you can visualize the future flow of steps and activities required to complete a project or activity.

_____

_____

_____

_____

_____

_____

_____

It's up to you to take care of yourself while meeting others' expectations.

Tell yourself that you can be all you want. That you can get things done and make time to spare. That you're absolutely determined to have more free time.

Plan ahead, anticipate where wait time may pop up, and use it wisely.

"You must learn to be still in the midst of activity and to be vibrantly alive in repose."

–Indira Gandhi

Your calendar is the most important visual reminder of your responsibilities. Keep it open and visible.

You can control your environment by limiting interruptions during periods when you have set your mind to getting something done.

In terms of time, the downside of succumbing to temptation is prolonging and complicating what needs to get done.

_____

_____

_____

_____

_____

_____

_____

_____

Always extend your time estimate of the time that's required to accomplish your goal. Do this for yourself as your own internal yardstick, and estimate time requirements for all the links in the chain.

You have a right to time for yourself. It's the passport to a well-balanced life. Wanting it is half the battle.

Little drops of water,
little grains of sand,
Make the mighty ocean,
and the pleasant land.
So the little minutes,
humble tho' they be,
Make the mighty ages of
Eternity.

–Julia Carney
"Little Things"

Waiting time can be a waste of time.

If things go wrong and your old habits seem to rise again, don't project into the future. Tell yourself today has been rough, but tomorrow will be better.

*You **can** have more time to enjoy life.*

_____

_____

_____

_____

_____

_____

_____

Think about what you want to change. If you don't
know how to, seek support by talking with friends,
relatives, religious advisors. Try spending some quiet
time alone. An insightful book may be helpful.

"We all live with the objective
of being happy. Our lives are
different and yet the same."

–Anne Frank

Add up the hours you think it will take to do a project under perfect conditions. Then estimate how long it will take if you are interrupted or swayed off course. Use the higher estimate and add in this fudge factor before you commit to a deadline.

Time is a limited asset—but an asset you can manage and control.

84

Anticipate waiting time and use it to your advantage. Have paper, pen, book, blank cards, tape recorder, etc. with you when you think you may be waiting.

_____

_____

_____

_____

_____

_____

_____

Recognize that when an interruption occurs, it steals your time without asking. Be kind to yourself, the person on the phone, or intruders, but be firm and keep to your schedule.

_____

_____

_____

_____

_____

_____

_____

Let a detailed calendar be the basis of your 'to do' list
for your personal and professional lives. Only make
commitments once you have reviewed it.

There is nothing wrong with
establishing a closed-door policy
for a given amount of time to help
you to get things done without
interruption.

"Let me tell thee, time is a very precious gift of God; so precious that He only gives it to us moment by moment. He would not have thee waste it."

–Amelia Barr

Fearing you will let someone down and avoiding commitment only breeds anxiety. Don't set yourself up to fail. Be confident. You'll come through.

Forgive yourself: it's a process.

Remember what's important.

_____

_____

_____

_____

_____

_____

_____

Once a week, sit down with your 'to do' lists and
review prior activities to see how you're doing.
Make sure you recognize the good you're doing.
Adjust your course as needed.

"Yet it is in our idleness, in our dreams, that the submerged truth sometimes comes to the top."

–Virginia Woolf
"A Room of One's Own"

Stop worrying about what you 'should' be doing by asking yourself: Did I plan to do it today? Is it a priority? Is it important? The more the answer is no, the more you will free yourself from the 'should' monster.

Learn to say no to others and yes to yourself.

List categories for your filing system. Choose a convenient
storage location, and find a storage method and updating
system that works for you.

If you really want to have free time, you'll get it.

Always ask yourself "What things that have to be done can only be done by me...not done best by me, but completed by me alone?" Delegate any items that don't need your personal attention.

The superwoman of the 80's is
extinct. The few who remain are
workaholic caretakers battling
heavy anxiety.

"One of the oddest things in life, I think, is the things one remembers."

–Agatha Christie

By listening effectively, you can determine what is
required and how much, if any, of your time is involved.

Learn how to break the mental pattern of believing "they need me" and "I can't say no."

To enjoy life and get things done, you must take a break. Make the time to relax, unwind, refocus, and recharge, even if it's only for fifteen minutes. You deserve it.

_____

_____

_____

_____

_____

_____

_____

'If it feels good, do it" is a very short-term approach to life.

Say yes to simplicity.

"Sometimes, I think
The things we see
Are shadows of the things to be;
That what we plan we build. . .

–Phoebe Cary
"Dreams and Realities"

Lighten up: make it fun.

It's up to you to want to enjoy life more. With your free time, you can choose to exercise, travel, think, nap, and even work. You're in control. It's your choice.

_____

_____

_____

_____

_____

_____

_____

The best way to learn to plan backwards is to develop a personal timeline of the past, present, and future.

118

_____

_____

_____

_____

_____

_____

_____

"Curious things, habits. People themselves never knew they had them."

-Agatha Christie

" . . .it is not merely the trivial which clutters our lives, but the important as well."

–Anne Morrow Lindbergh

Serenity Prayer:

"God grant me the serenity to accept the things I cannot change. Courage to change the things I can. . .
And wisdom to know the difference."

Time is a gift you give yourself.

Make time to waste time. Put a limit on it, but when you want to vegetate, go ahead. Do absolutely nothing. Consider it a luxury you deserve.

"When people say, 'she's got everything,' I've only one answer: I haven't had tomorrow."
-Elizabeth Taylor

_____

_____

_____

_____

_____

_____

_____

Don't make promises until you thoroughly understand what you have to do, what impact the promise will have on your other commitments, and the importance of the promise to your own goals.

"Those whom we support hold us up in life."

–Marie Ebner von Eshenbach

"Without discipline, there's no life at all."

−Katherine Hepburn

Write down how you would like to feel, and where you would like to be spending more of your time.

Perception is reality.

Expect the unexpected at all times.

_____

_____

_____

_____

_____

_____

_____

You can get many things done by phoning instead of driving around to a store or waiting in traffic.

"You must do the thing you think you cannot do."

—Eleanor Roosevelt

I too am a rare
Pattern.
As I wander down
The garden paths.

         –Amy Lowell
           "Patterns"

Create memories by scheduling personal time for you.

Keep clocks on the walls and always wear a watch. Seeing time tick away will motivate you to use it to your best advantage.

The first step to simplifying your life is to recognize the importance of simple things and precious moments.

You are capable of doing two or even three things at once. When you do, you make more time—time to do with as you may.

"It is good to have an end to journey towards; but it is the journey that matters in the end."

–Ursula K. Le Guin

One by one the sands are flowing,

One by one the moments fall;

Some are coming, some are going;

Do not strive to grasp them all.

—Adelaide Proctor
"One by One"

Winning isn't everything. Attitude is.

While we all want to feel needed, there comes a time when you have to stop doing for others and let others learn to care for themselves.

149

Slow down and enjoy your journey through this wonderful life.

_____

_____

_____

_____

_____

_____

_____

We have to decide what is most important, what comes next, what can wait. The priority is based on each person's perception of the consequences of each activity.

151

"Honesty is a selfish virtue. Yes, I am honest enough."

–Gertrude Stein

"A little kingdom I possess,
	where thought and feelings
	dwell;
And very hard the task I find
	of governing it well."

		–Louisa May Alcott
		"My Kingdom"

Sometimes solitude is all it takes to discover answers to nagging questions.